Write It Right

Writing a Letter

By Cecilia Minden and Kate Roth

Published in the United States of America by
Cherry Lake Publishing
Ann Arbor, Michigan
www.cherrylakepublishing.com

Reading Adviser: Marla Conn MS, Ed., Literacy specialist, Read-Ability, Inc.
Book Designer: Felicia Macheske
Character Illustrator: Carol Herring

Photo Credits: @ Stephanie Frey/Shutterstock, 7; © Shchus/Shutterstock, 9; wizdata1/Shutterstock, 11; © Galleria Laureata/Shutterstock, 15; © Cheryl Casey/Shutterstock, 17

Graphics Throughout: © simple surface/Shutterstock.com; © Mix3r/Shutterstock.com; © Artefficient/Shutterstock.com; © lemony/Shutterstock.com; © Svetolk/Shutterstock.com; © EV-DA/Shutterstock.com; © briddy/Shutterstock.com; © IreneArt/Shutterstock.com

Copyright © 2020 by Cherry Lake Publishing
All rights reserved. No part of this book may be reproduced or utilized in any form or by any means without written permission from the publisher.

Library of Congress Cataloging-in-Publication Data

Names: Minden, Cecilia, author. | Roth, Kate, author. | Herring, Carol, illustrator.
Title: Writing a letter / by Cecilia Minden and Kate Roth ; illustrated by Carol Herring.
Description: Ann Arbor : Cherry Lake Publishing, [2019] | Series: Write it right | Includes bibliographical references and index.
Identifiers: LCCN 2019006004| ISBN 9781534147157 (hardcover) | ISBN 9781534148581 (pdf) | ISBN 9781534150010 (pbk.) | ISBN 9781534151444 (hosted ebook)
Subjects: LCSH: Letter writing—Juvenile literature. | English language—Composition and exercises—Juvenile literature.
Classification: LCC PE1483 .M56 2019 | DDC 808.6—dc23
LC record available at https://lccn.loc.gov/2019006004

Cherry Lake Publishing would like to acknowledge the work of The Partnership for 21st Century Skills.
Please visit *www.p21.org* for more information.

Printed in the United States of America
Corporate Graphics

Table of CONTENTS

CHAPTER ONE
A Friendly Letter 4

CHAPTER TWO
Greetings! 8

CHAPTER THREE
Read All About It! 10

CHAPTER FOUR
P.S. Sign Your Name 14

CHAPTER FIVE
The Envelope, Please 16

CHAPTER SIX
Ready to Mail 18

GLOSSARY 22
FOR MORE INFORMATION 23
INDEX 24
ABOUT THE AUTHORS 24

CHAPTER ONE

A Friendly Letter

Did you ever get a letter in the mail? It is fun to have someone send a letter to you. You can write a letter too. Think how happy a friend or loved one would be to get a letter from you. Let's get started!

It is exciting to get a letter in the mail.

A letter has five main points:

1. HEADING
(the letter writer's address and the date)

2. GREETING
(the words that begin a letter)

3. BODY
(the main part of a letter)

4. CLOSING
(the words that end a letter)

5. SIGNATURE
(the letter writer's name, written by hand)

474 Spring Street
Anytown, State 01010
July 10, 2019

Dear Riley,

Are you coming to the beach this year? I hope all of our other cousins come too.

We will be there in two weeks. Grandma and Grandpa said this year will be extra special. Do you think they have a surprise planned? What do you think it could be?

Mom helped me sew a bag to use when I collect shells. I could make one for you. What color would you like?

Please write to me. I would like to hear from you.

Your cousin,
Ella

P.S. I hope we can have a bonfire on the beach like we did last year.

Stationery is used for writing letters. Sometimes they come in a special size or design. Sometimes they even come with matching **envelopes**. But almost any kind of paper and envelope will work.

Here's what you'll need to complete the activities in this book:

- Notebook paper
- Stationery and envelope
- Stamp
- Pencil with an eraser
- Pen
- **Dictionary**

Gather together everything you will need.

CHAPTER TWO

Greetings!

Who will get your letter? This helps you decide what you will write. Maybe your uncle lives in another city. You want him to be your pen pal. This is someone who writes to you and you write back to him or her.

Grab a pencil and a sheet of notebook paper or stationery. Let's start writing a letter!

The first step is choosing a pen pal.

ACTIVITY

Heading and Greeting

INSTRUCTIONS:

1. Use the letter on page 5 as a model for your letter.
2. Write the heading. The first part of the heading is your home address. It goes in the top left corner of the page.
3. Write today's date below your address.
4. Now write the greeting "Dear" and the person's name.
5. Put a comma after the person's name.

It's time for the next step of writing a letter.

CHAPTER THREE

Read All About It!

Your news goes in the body of the letter. What news would you like to share? What would the person you are writing to enjoy reading?

Grab a separate sheet of notebook paper. Make a short list of ideas for your letter. Here are some examples:

- A movie you enjoyed watching
- Trying out for the track team ✓
- Your volunteer time at the pet shelter ✓

You could write about a video game you like to play.

Include pictures you would like to share.

ACTIVITY

Body

INSTRUCTIONS:

1. Choose two ideas from your list.
2. Write two or three sentences about each idea. These sentences will become a **paragraph**.
3. You can also write questions. Your pen pal will answer the questions when he or she writes back.
4. Work on your sentences until they are just right. Use a dictionary to check your spelling.

Now you have the body of your letter. What do you think comes next?

1. PET SHELTER:

Dad and I are now volunteering at the animal shelter two Saturdays a month. We help the animals get used to being with people. My favorite part is taking the animals on walks. Do you have a pet? Do you take your pet on walks?

2. TRACK TRYOUTS:

I'm going to try out for the track team. Dad said you were a track star. What event did you like the best?

CHAPTER FOUR

P.S. Sign Your Name

The closing is how you say goodbye. There are many different closings. Choose one you like.

Write your signature below the closing. Sign only your first name if you know the person well.

Did you forget something? Add a **postscript**, or P.S. This is a short message that goes below your name.

ACTIVITY

Closing and Signature

INSTRUCTIONS:

1. Choose a closing for your letter. Here are some examples:

   - Hugs,
   - Smiles,
   - Have a nice day,

2. Make sure the first letter of the first word is uppercase. The rest of the words should be lowercase.

3. Put a comma at the end of the closing.

4. Sign your name below the closing.

5. If needed, add a P.S. below your signed name.

You can have fun thinking up clever closings.

CHAPTER FIVE

The Envelope, Please

Your letter is finished! All that is left is to put it in an envelope. There are post offices all over the world. They take care of a lot of mail. Help them by making sure everything on the envelope is correct.

Make sure the stamp is secure.

ACTIVITY

Addressing an Envelope

INSTRUCTIONS:

1. Position the envelope so the **seal flap** is at the top.
2. Be sure to write on the front of the envelope.
3. Write your name and address in the upper left corner.
4. Write the name and address of the person getting the letter in the center of the envelope.
5. Put a stamp in the upper right corner.

• •

Postal codes and stamps are different all over the world. You can find other postal codes by visiting World Postal Codes (https://worldpostalcode.com). An adult can help you find the code.

Always use a pen when you address an envelope.

CHAPTER SIX

Ready to Mail

ACTIVITY

Check your letter and envelope one more time!

Ask yourself these questions as you reread your letter:

1. Did I write a heading in the upper left corner?
2. Did I use the greeting "Dear"?
3. Did I spell the person's name correctly?
4. Did I remember a comma after the name?
5. Is the body of the letter clear and easy to understand?
6. Did I spell all words correctly?
7. Did I include a closing?
8. Is the closing more than one word? If so, does only the first word begin with a capital letter?

ACTIVITY
—Continued—

9. Did I remember the comma with the closing?
10. Did I sign my name?
11. Does the envelope have my address and the reader's address?
12. Is there a stamp in the top right corner?

Did you answer yes to all of the questions? Good job!

You are nearly ready to mail your letter!

474 Spring Street
Anytown, State 01010
August 14, 2019

Dear Uncle Zeke,

How do you like being in the navy? Do you go out to sea on big boats? I think you look great in your uniform.

Dad and I are now volunteering at the animal shelter two Saturdays a month. We help the animals get used to being with people. My favorite part is taking the animals on walks.

I'm going to try out for the track team. Dad said you were a track star. What event did you like the best?

Please write me back, Uncle Zeke. We can be pen pals.

Hugs,

Ella

P.S. Are you coming home soon? I sure miss you!

Did you include all the parts in your letter?

Now, put your letter in the envelope. Seal it shut. Don't forget to mail the letter! It won't take too long to reach the reader. Soon, you may find a letter in the mail just for you!

Everyone is happy to get a letter just for them!

GLOSSARY

dictionary (DIK-shuh-ner-ee) a book that lists words and their meanings

envelopes (AHN-vuh-lopes) flat paper coverings that are used to mail letters

paragraph (PAIR-uh-graf) a group of sentences about a certain idea or subject

postscript (POHST-skript) a message that begins with "P.S." and is added to a letter below the writer's signed name

seal flap (SEEL FLAP) the part of an envelope that folds down to close it

stationery (STAY-shuh-ner-ee) special paper used for letter writing

For More INFORMATION

BOOKS

Capici, Gaetano. *How Did That Get to My House? Mail.* Ann Arbor, MI: Cherry Lake Publishing, 2010.

Loewen, Nancy. *Sincerely Yours: Writing Your Own Letter.* Minneapolis, MN: Picture Window Books, 2009.

WEBSITE

PBS Kids: Arthur—Letter Writer Helper
http://grownups.pbskids.org/arthur/games/letterwriter/letter.html
Look here to learn more about the parts of a letter.

INDEX

address, 17

body, 5, 10–13

closing, 5, 14–15

envelopes, 6, 16–17

good-bye, 14

greeting, 5, 8–9

heading, 5, 8–9

letter
  ideas for, 10
  mailing, 16–19, 21
  main parts, 5
  sample, 20
  what it is, 4–7

mailing, 16–19, 21

news, 10–11

paragraph, 12
pen pal, 8
postscript (P.S.), 14

questions, 12

signature, 5, 14, 15
stationery, 6

About the AUTHORS

Cecilia Minden is the former director of the Language and Literacy Program at Harvard Graduate School of Education. She earned her doctorate from the University of Virginia. Her research focused on early literacy skills. She is currently a literacy consultant and the author of over 100 books for children. Dr. Minden lives with her family in McKinney, Texas. She loves to spend time reading books and writing to family and friends.

Kate Roth has a doctorate from Harvard University in language and literacy and a master's degree from Columbia University Teachers College in curriculum and teaching. Her work focuses on writing instruction in the primary grades. She has taught kindergarten, first grade, and Reading Recovery. She has also instructed hundreds of teachers from around the world in early literacy practices. She lived with her husband and three children in China for many years, and now they live in Connecticut.